Family Recovery
Growing Beyond Addiction

by Merlene Miller and Terence T. Gorski

Herald House/Independence Press
P.O. Box HH
3225 South Noland Road
Independence, Missouri 64055
1-800-767-8181

Dedicated To
Fran Kohler

CONTENTS

INTRODUCTION

Society has given concerned persons no rules or guidelines with which to deal with alcoholism in the family. With the crisis of alcoholism, the traditional tools of family problem solving and crisis reaction don't work. The family reacts in the only way they know, by using the only tools society has given to deal with problems and family crises.

What happens to the concerned persons in an alcoholic family is a normal and natural response to the disease process of alcoholism. Families are made dysfunctional by the attempt to cope with alcoholism in the only way they know; but when they are unable to function due to a lack of guidelines and of coping skills, they are often blamed for their own dysfunction and for perpetuating the disease process of alcoholism. They are unable to function because they lack knowledge and skills.

There are strengths that families of alcoholics develop that allow them to survive in spite of the crisis of alcoholism. They develop their own ways of coping. While these strengths allow them to continue to survive in spite of their problem, the problem of alcoholism is intensified. Normal problem-solving responses result in problem intensification. The normal reaction within any family to pain, to crisis, and to dysfunction of one member of the family is to reduce pain, ease crisis, and to assist the dysfunctional member in order to protect the family.

These normal responses to problems and crisis allow the alcoholic to escape the painful consequences of drinking. Pain is nature's way of teaching us that we are ill and that we need help. The alcoholic, thus deprived of painful learning experiences, is also deprived of the opportunity to experience the awareness of alcohol as the problem in his or her life.

As the normal means of coping fail to work for the family, they try harder. They try to be more supportive, more helpful, more understanding. They begin to doubt their own value as persons. After all, they have failed in the role of wife, husband, or parent. They try harder. They take on the responsibilities of the alcoholic, not realizing that this causes the alcoholic to become irresponsible.

The family experiences frustration, anxiety, guilt, and self-pity. These are normal results of repeated failure. The family does what they do out of a sincere desire to help the alcoholic and to maintain the family. As the things they do in a sincere effort to help, don't help; as their best efforts at solutions fail and tend to make things worse; the family begins to develop its own sick reaction and response to the disease process of alcoholism. They have tried what religion, society, and our culture has taught them. It doesn't work, and the resulting despair and guilt bring about confusion and chaos. As the alcoholic must be viewed as a victim of a disease, so must the characteristics of the concerned persons be viewed as a reaction to the progressive stress of the disease. Their behavior has a very immediate motivation, stabilization of the family. In the context of what is best for the alcoholic, behavior of a concerned person may be dysfunctional; but in the context of the rest of the family, the behavior might appear quite functional.

At this point the family members may recognize that

they need help. But nothing will help until they learn new ways to cope, until they learn some ways of responding to alcoholism that can interrupt the dysfunctional process that is occurring. Recognizing the need for help is the first step. There are three things that have to happen before a dysfunctional family can become functional. They must recognize that they have become dysfunctional. They must have hope that things can be different. They must take action to start the change process.

The spouse can recover even if the alcoholic continues to drink. It is not easy. It is kind of like operating a guillotine. You have to be able to keep your head while everyone else is losing theirs.

In order to recover, the family has to learn that there are things that can be changed and things that can't. Learning to tell the difference is a big step in recovery. If you can't tell the difference, you may spend your life beating your head against the wall trying to change what you can't do anything about and ignoring what you can.

Some people go from one extreme to another, first trying to change everything and then getting so locked into acceptance that they stop believing that anything can be different. Some people feel such despair that they give up hope that things can ever be different or that they should be different. They begin to believe that this is their lot in life.

In order to recover there must be hope. The focus has to change from the alcoholic and drinking behavior to self. Before anything can be done for the alcoholic, the spouse must develop personal strengths. He or she may need to learn to stop being giving, forgiving, sacrificing, protective, and most of all, responsible for the alcoholic.

He or she may have to learn new ways to be supportive and caring.

This book is intended as a guide for recovering family members. It is intended to guide them in understanding alcoholism, understanding their own reactions to the disease process of alcoholism, building their own personal strengths, developing skills to interrupt alcoholism and motivate the alcoholic to seek treatment, and to provide skills for restructuring the family unit.

UNDERSTANDING ALCOHOLISM

The first step in recovery for the family is education about the disease of alcoholism. Before you can look at yourself and see what is wrong, you have to understand what is at the heart of the problem. You have to have a deep-down belief and acceptance that alcoholism is a disease. When you can come to understand and accept it as a true disease, you are better able to let go of resentments, bitterness, guilt, and defensiveness. You will be better able to view the alcoholic's response to the disease as a normal part of the disease. And then you will be able to view your own responses as normal. You can see your own illness with less guilt and less defensiveness.

There are things you can change and things you cannot change, and you must learn to distinguish between the two. There are things about the disease of alcoholism that you cannot change, and the more you know about the disease, the more you will recognize what those things are.

A PRIMARY DISEASE

Alcoholism is a disease. It is a primary disease. This means that it is the original disease, not the result of another disease. If it were caused by another disease it would be called a secondary disease. Cirrhosis of the liver, for example, is a secondary disease which results from the primary disease of alcoholism. You should not confuse the resulting condition with the primary disease. Sometimes people get treatment for the conditions resulting from alcoholism and believe they are getting treatment for their primary problem. It does no good to treat the secondary conditions until the alcoholism is under control. No effective or lasting healing of damaged body organs will take place until alcohol is removed from the body. Sobriety is the necessary first step of treatment.

Alcoholism is not the result of drinking too much. Drinking too much is the result of alcoholism. The body of the alcoholic does not react to alcohol in the same way that the body of a nonalcoholic does. Alcoholics are *powerless* over the way their bodies react to alcohol.

There is much evidence that alcoholism is hereditary. It does run in families, and it is very likely that it is inherited in the same way that eye color is inherited. The color of your eyes has nothing to do with morality or character, mental processes or choice. Neither does inheriting alcoholism.

Let's look at how the body of an alcoholic is powerless over alcohol. The body of an alcoholic responds to alcohol differently than the body of a nonalcoholic. We don't know all the reasons why that happens, but there are certain things we do know.

Alcohol is a sedative drug. A sedative drug is one that calms or quiets the nervous system and causes a person to feel relaxed. The nonalcoholic will usually feel relaxed and become drowsy after several drinks. But something different happens in the alcoholic. There is a feeling of agitation that develops after the first drinks that creates an urgency to drink more. The alcoholic is *powerless* over this compulsion.

As alcoholics continue to drink, the feeling of agitation

is relieved. They have a period of control-level drinking when they feel better, behave better, and do not appear intoxicated in spite of high blood alcohol levels. These people often take pride in being able to "hold their liquor." This is *tolerance,* and in the early stage of alcoholism there is an increase in tolerance. The cells of the liver change to adapt to the higher levels of alcohol. As the liver changes to tolerate higher levels of alcohol, a dependence develops. There is no longer just a tolerance for alcohol but a need for alcohol. Drinking no longer occurs because of want but because of need.

The liver has adapted or changed to accommodate increased levels of alcohol, and the change creates a dependence or a need for alcohol. Alcoholics are not aware of the developing need for alcohol. They are usually in control, feel good while drinking, function better than when sober. If the alcoholic drinks beyond the level of control, there is loss of control of behavior. Profound intoxication, agitation, nervousness, or perhaps violence may occur.

Alcoholics are powerless to control the way their bodies react to alcohol. They are powerless over the body's responses to alcohol and over the ability to control drinking behavior. Alcoholics are powerless over alcohol and so are the people who love them. The alcoholic did not cause it. Step One in the Alanon Twelve Steps states: "We admitted we were powerless over alcohol, that our lives had become unmanageable." This is something you cannot change. This is something you can't control.

A CHRONIC DISEASE

Alcoholism is a chronic disease. Chronic diseases are those which come on gradually over a period of time. This is different from acute disease. Acute diseases come on rapidly; you may be well one day and very ill the next. Chronic disease progresses slowly so that there may be a long period between being well and realizing that you are ill. It develops gradually so that the alcoholic and family are able to develop physical, psychological, behavioral, and social ways to live with the disease. Because this happens slowly over a period of time, neither alcoholics nor their families are aware that they have compensated for and adapted to their illness. They are able to deny that they are sick for a long time.

Because alcoholism is a chronic disease, there is a high risk of relapse; there is always the danger that it may recur. It is never cured. It can only be controlled. Unless measures are taken on a long-term basis to control the disease, relapse is likely. Most alcoholics return to drinking at least once after they make the decision to stop. For many it is a way of life. "It will never happen again," and then it does. The family believes that every time is the last time.

The family reacts to alcoholism as an acute disease. Each crisis is an isolated event that will never happen again. The normal response to acute crisis is to minimize the consequences. This is counterproductive to recovery from alcoholism.

Because alcoholism can only be arrested, not cured, the alcoholic cannot expect to resume drinking. Alcohol will reactivate the symptoms of the disease at any time.

Total abstinence is necessary to control alcoholism, but abstinence is not the only requirement. Remember that the alcoholic has developed a way of life to accommodate the illness. Because it takes a long time to get sick, it takes a long time to recover. Recovery requires long-term total treatment which promotes physical, psychological, behavioral, and social recovery. A promise to stop drinking is not the solution. The alcoholic cannot recover without help, without treatment of some kind. Treatment may be hospitalization, private counseling, Alcoholics Anonymous, or a variety of other treatment programs. The family must recognize that a promise to quit drinking, however sincerely made, cannot be kept by the alcoholic without treatment.

Each crisis that occurs within the family because of alcoholism is part of a chronic, ongoing disease process. To view each crisis as an isolated event, to believe that it will never happen again, is to set yourself up for repeated disappointment, frustration, anger, or even rejection. To view each crisis as part of an ongoing process is to accept alcoholism as a chronic disease and to develop the skills to be able to use crisis as an opportunity for recovery.

A PROGRESSIVE DISEASE

Alcoholism is a progressive disease. It always gets worse without treatment. It never gets better; it never stays the same. As it progresses it affects all areas of life — physical, psychological, behavioral, and social — and the life of the alcoholic becomes unmanageable. Alcoholism progresses through three stages: the early stage, the middle stage, and the chronic stage.

The early stage is marked by increased tolerance. Increased tolerance means that the alcoholic is able to drink more and more and not become drunk. The alcoholic can drink large quantities of alcohol and behavior improves. The alcohol helps him feel better about himself, have more confidence, and demonstrate a higher level of social skills. As the disease progresses, the alcoholic is seeking to recover the good feelings of the early stage, but once it is gone it can never be recaptured.

The middle stage of alcoholism is marked by a progressive loss of control over drinking and a decrease in tolerance. Tolerance becomes dependence; want becomes need. As the liver cells change in order to tolerate large quantities of alcohol, the change creates a need for the alcohol. As the dependence increases, the alcoholic has less and less control over drinking and drinking behavior. There is a progressive loss of control in three different ways: loss of control over the beginning of drinking episodes, over behavior during drinking episodes, and over the end of drinking episodes.

Alcoholics become less able to choose not to take the first drink. More and more often they find themselves behaving while drinking in ways they would not choose while sober, and as tolerance decreases, the loss of control occurs earlier in the drinking episodes. It takes fewer drinks before the person goes beyond the control level and experiences symptoms of intoxication.

The chronic stage of alcoholism is marked by deterioration. The main deterioration is physical. Alcoholics develop organ system diseases such as liver disease, heart disease, gastrointestinal problems, malnutrition, and muscle problems. They also develop neurological problems; that is, impairment in the brain and the central nervous system. This results in thought process, emotional process, and memory impairments. There is also psychological deterioration. These are problems related to thinking and feeling. Some of the psychological effects of alcoholism are a deteriorated self-image, depression, anxiety, unreasonable fears, rigid denial, possible destructive behavior, and a change in values. As a result, problems in behavior begin to occur. The alcholic begins to lose problem-solving abilities, life-planning skills, and performance skills. Behavior becomes self-defeating.

Behavioral problems result in social problems. Because of fear and anxiety and guilt, the alcoholic begins to isolate from family and friends. There is a loss of communication skills. There are strained personal relationships, and eventually work habits become unreliable and sporadic.

It must be remembered that alcoholism never gets better and it never stays the same. Many times the family develops coping skills and comes to believe that they can handle the situation just as it is. However, the situation will not stay as it is. It will always get worse. Delayed treatment may be too late. Early intervention means more likelihood of recovery and more possibility of full recovery for the alcoholic and the family.

PHYSICAL EFFECTS

All body systems are affected by the progression of alcoholism. There is damage throughout the body as alcoholism gets worse. At first the damage is acute and temporary. Then damage becomes chronic and permanent. Acute damage means there is inflamation in the organ systems. This can be repaired. Eventually the inflamed cells and tissues die and are replaced by scar tissue. This is permanent damage that cannot be repaired.

Acute conditions: headaches, impaired thought and emotional processes, chest pain, hypertension, respiratory infections, gastritis, pancreatitis, hepatitis, fatty liver, poor muscle tone, bladder infections.

Chronic conditions: stroke, "wet brain" (permanent brain damage), heart attack, arteriosclerosis, varicose veins in the esophagus, cirrhosis of the liver, damage to heart muscles, bone marrow depression (where blood cells are made), kidney failure, impotence, sterility.

These are only a few of the physical complications of alcoholism. Every body system is affected. Many times the body repairs itself. The earlier that alcoholism is arrested, the more possibility there is for full recovery.

PSYCHOLOGICAL EFFECTS

As alcoholism progresses, there are personality changes in the alcoholic. Psychological problems do not cause alcoholism, but alcoholism causes psychological problems. There are a number of reasons why these changes and problems occur.

As a result of the neurological impairments (damage to brain and central nervous system) that occur with alcoholism, alcoholics begin to see themselves differently than they did before. They also begin to see other people and the world around them in a different way. Because of the need to protect drinking, beliefs and values change or seem to change. Guilt feelings, mood swings, depression develop. They begin blaming others for their problems because it is too painful to blame themselves and because blaming themselves might mean giving up alcohol. They believe they must have alcohol to survive.

In order to cope with a reality too painful to face and because they *must* protect their drinking, they refuse to admit anything is wrong. This is called denial. It is not concious lying. They convince themselves it is really true.

Denial is increased because of neurological impairments that distort reality and cause blackouts. Alcoholics cannot remember what happened during blackouts and this makes it easier to deny the reality of what is happening. *Denial of the disease is part of the disease.*

Understanding that denial is part of the disease can help you cope with some of the unreasonable behavior of the alcoholic. Denial blocks the motivation for recovery by blocking the painful reality of alcoholism. The family can help motivate recovery by not blocking the pain necessary for the alcoholic to become aware of the disease process taking place.

BEHAVIORAL EFFECTS

Alcoholics cannot control their behavior and no family member can control the behavior of an alcoholic. Alcoholics do what they do because of the effect of the disease on their behavior. Until there is treatment it is counterproductive for family members to attempt to control the behavior of the alcoholic.

In the early stages alcoholics drink to improve behavior and performance. Eventually they use alcohol just in an effort to function normally. Much of what alcoholics have learned has been while drinking. Those things are always affected by *state dependent learning*. What they have learned while drinking they will recall most easily at the same blood alcohol level. Without alcohol they are unable to perform tasks that were easily performed while drinking. As alcohol is used with more and more life activities, alcoholics become *powerless* to function without it.

As drinking becomes more and more important, alcoholics have less control over their behavior. Life is consumed by the need to drink. Anything that interferes with drinking becomes unimportant.

When drinking becomes more important than anything else, alcoholics begin to violate their own value systems. While drinking they do things they would not do sober. While sober they structure their lives to protect their drinking. They break promises, forget commitments, lie, all to protect drinking.

SOCIAL EFFECTS

Alcoholism is social. The effects of alcoholism are far reaching. They aren't limited to the physical, psychological, and behavioral deterioration of the alcoholic. The lives of the people the alcoholic lives with, works with, and associates with are affected. As life becomes more alcohol centered, alcoholics isolate themselves from other people. They give up social activities that were important to them because the activities interfere with their drinking. Friends and acquaintances separate themselves from the alcoholic because his/her behavior becomes embarrassing or offensive. The family withdraws from social contacts out of fear of what the alcoholic may do. Children stop bringing their friends around; the spouse doesn't invite people to the house. Communication skills are lost as the alcoholic withdraws to drink alone.

As the behavior of alcoholics results in more and more crises and as they become more unable to fulfill their roles in their families, other family members take over their responsibilities. If John has handled family finances and begins to bounce checks, someone else will take over the job. If he neglects his responsibilities around the house or with the car, someone else will begin doing his jobs. If Alice is too drunk to care for the baby, an older child may do it. The alcoholic allows this, even welcomes it (after all it leaves more times to drink), but at the same time may resent this dependency and find other ways to be dominant. Attempts to be assertive may lead to aggression, unreasonable demands, verbal abuse, or physical violence.

There is no consistency or dependability in any area of family life. Broken promises, unfulfilled expectations and disrupted plans create tension and strained relationships. Family members are isolated and separated from one another by fear, anger, and confusion. Disruption of the family increases with the progression of the disease of alcoholism. The entire family needs help to rebuild trust, reestablish communication, and learn how to feel good about themselves.

The job is usually the last aspect of the alcoholic's life to be affected by alcohol-related behavior. Because alcoholics value and need their jobs, they struggle to protect them and separate them from drinking as long as possible. But eventually they can no longer draw the line and drinking invades the last unaffected area in spite of their efforts. Absenteeism, tardiness, accidents, and low productivity lead to conflicts with supervisors, co-workers, and subordinates and eventually put the job in jeopardy. Deterioration of this last area is often what motivates the alcoholic to seek treatment.

As these things occur a family member may begin to feel *if he loved me, he wouldn't do these things.* But it must be remembered that alcoholics' behavior has nothing to do with caring about their families. They do not choose what is happening. Their lives have become unmanageable.

UNDERSTANDING YOUR RESPONSE TO ALCOHOLISM

Alcoholism constitutes unique and predictable stressors upon the family and thus creates unique disturbances within the family unit. The disease creates impairment in alcoholics that makes it impossible for them to respond appropriately to the needs of the family system. There is a natural tendency for the family to compensate for this inappropriate behavior in order to keep the family functioning. They develop their own survival systems. They adapt and condition themselves to a new system of functioning that allows the family to maintain itself in the midst of chaos and confusion. They develop strengths that allow them to survive in spite of the crisis of alcoholism. But these strengths do not interrupt the disease process going on in the family and they reduce the pain only momentarily. In fact, behavior that keeps the family functioning may be what perpetuates the problem. The progression of disease and the progression of family disruption will continue until family members learn new ways to respond to the stress of alcoholism in the family.

PSYCHOLOGICAL EFFECTS

In the early stages of alcoholism, the family usually does not recognize the problem. They know something is wrong, but they don't know what it is. They blame other things for their problems — job-related stress, in-laws, money, sex, children. They try everything they know to solve these problems and nothing works. Everyone has to make sense out of life. When the things you have been taught don't work and you don't know anything else to try, defense mechanisms help to make sense out of life. Defenses are an attempt to change reality to what we want it to be. Defenses keep the family functioning through confusion and chaos. They keep family members functioning in the midst of a reality too painful to face.

Sometimes family members are able to convince themselves that there really is no problem. They keep on functioning as though everything is all right and refuse to look at or deal with the actual situation. Sometimes they avoid the problem. If drinking has become a problem at parties, the spouse may just refuse to go to parties with the alcoholic or may avoid the problem by just not talking about it. Sometimes the family excuses the behavior of the drinking person. They convince themselves that everyone drinks; everyone gets drunk once in a while; it's New Year's Eve; it probably won't happen again; it's just the pressure of the job; she's just lonely. Sometimes spouses of alcoholics take the responsibility on themselves. They come to believe that if they were better wives or better husbands, if they controlled the children better, if they watched the budget better, if they were home more, that the drinking person wouldn't have a problem.

Although the use of defense mechanisms perpetuates the disease of alcoholism, the family cannot break through them constructively without help to find new ways to respond to the problem. Defense mechanisms protect the family and enable them to continue to function.

As the family begins to recognize the problem, they

usually try to hide it. Embarrassment, fear, and anger become a part of life. Spouses who have tried everything they know to solve the problems as they see them feel frustrated and guilty. They believe there must be something more that could have been done and have a strong sense of failure. They begin to develop fears of what might happen next and anxiety that they are unable to identify. Family members blame one another. Fear, lack of trust, guilt, resentment, and blaming get out of control and replace good feelings the family may once have had.

PHYSICAL EFFECTS

The emotional stress of living with alcoholism is registered in the body. There is a physical response to fear, to anxiety, to guilt, to self-pity, to worry. The body reacts with stress-related illnesses such as high blood pressure, migraine headaches, gastrointestinal distress, breathing difficulties, ulcers, and weight problems.

The family members come to believe that the physical problems are the primary problems, and they seek relief through pain relievers and medical help. Usually the medical profession does not recognize the cause of the stress-related illness and treats the symptom without discovering the primary problem. The illnesses in the family increase tension and worry and place additional pressure on family members.

BEHAVIORAL EFFECTS

Eventually the family may become as obsessed with the alcoholism as the alcoholic, even when they are not able to identify or recognize alcoholism as the source of their problems. Behavior of family members is weighed in light of behavior of the alcoholic. There is an attempt to control drinking and drinking situations. They believe that if they can only control the drinking, everything will be all right. Many methods are used to control drinking. A husband may drink with his wife in order to control how much she drinks. A wife may cancel social events where heavy drinking is likely to occur. They may pour out liquor, hide liquor, or dilute liquor. They may attempt to control the money so that the money isn't available for alcohol. They may plead, demand, threaten, or beg, all in an effort to control when, where, how much, or how often the alcoholic drinks.

When family members are unable to control the quantity, time, or place of drinking, they may try to control the reasons for drinking. They may believe that the alcoholic works too hard and try to get him to slow down. They may feel that he isn't getting enough rest, isn't getting enough love, doesn't eat right, and change their own behavior to accommodate the needs of the alcoholic. Children may come to believe that drinking occurs because of them and modify their own behavior. A wife may try to make herself more sexually attractive to remedy sexual problems that are a result of the drinking.

Attempting to eliminate the problems by eliminating the reasons they believe the drinking occurs, doesn't eliminate the problem. The alcoholic does not drink because of working too hard, not eating right, not getting enough rest, or because the kids make him nervous. Drinking occurs because of dependence or addiction and cannot be controlled by the alcoholic or the family. When family members are unable to control drinking or the reasons for drinking, they attempt to control the consequences of drinking behavior. This is called *enabling.* Enabling makes it easier for the alcoholic to continue drinking. Drinking is easier because enabling behavior protects the alcoholic from pain. Enabling behavior is not intended to protect the alcoholic as much as to protect the family, but the alcoholic is protected and consequently can go on drinking.

In an effort to protect the family from embarrassment, financial insecurity, pain, or disruption, family members may make excuses, buy into the alcoholic's alibis, or cover up for the alcoholic. A wife may call an employer to say that her husband is sick when he really has a hangover. He doesn't have to face a painful situation. A husband may cover bad checks that his wife wrote while drinking. Parents may pay a lawyer to beat a DUI charge for a teenager.

The alcoholic can deny the problem as long as the family provides an escape from the consequences and doesn't allow association between the pain and the drinking. Enabling is a sincere effort to help, to spare the alcoholic pain and to preserve the family from further disintegration.

The family sees each alcohol-related problem as a separate isolated event rather than a chronic ongoing condition. They believe if they can get over this crisis everything is going to be all right. Once the crisis is over, they bury everything until the next crisis. They don't talk about it; they don't think about it. They don't realize that alcoholism is chronic and will keep recurring until it is treated. They don't know that alcoholism is a progressive disease that always gets worse and never gets better without treatment. They react to each crisis as an isolated incident that will be over and done with if they can just control the consequences this once so that as few people as possible are hurt.

SOCIAL EFFECTS

When family life becomes painful, chaotic, and unpredictable because of drinking behavior, the family reorganizes itself around new roles, new rules, and new rituals that protect it from disintegration.

As resentments develop in the family, productive communication may cease to exist. Family members withdraw from one another because of the pain of interaction, and they withdraw from people outside the family because of the fear of exposure. There is no consistency or dependability in any area of family life.

A SECONDARY CONDITION

The illness that develops in family members is not a primary condition. It is a normal response to the primary disease of alcoholism. There are not psychiatric disorders going on. Until the family members recognize the source of the family dysfunction and disintegration and learn new ways to respond to the disease of alcoholism, they will not be able to interrupt the illness processes going on in their own lives.

A CHRONIC CONDITION

The family illness does not end with the recovery of the alcoholic. Once this process has been set in motion it becomes a chronic condition that requires treatment. Getting treatment for the alcoholic is not enough. Nor is separation from the alcoholic the answer. Treatment for family members is necessary for their own recovery and, like alcoholism, their illness is subject to relapse. Fear, anger, guilt, resentments, and anxiety, if not treated, may be controlled temporarily but may be triggered at any time so that they become unmanageable. Before the family members are able to focus on the recovery of the family unit, they must focus on their individual recovery and build personal strengths. Private counseling, group treatment, or Al-Anon can facilitate recovery.

A PROGRESSIVE CONDITION

Without treatment the family illness will get worse. Fear, anxiety, guilt, and resentment will progress, from being uncomfortable to being totally out of control. Severe depression may result or a sense of total hopelessness and loss of self-worth. They may feel they are going insane or experience total physical, emotional, social, and spiritual deterioration.

UNDERSTANDING THE RESPONSE OF CHILDREN TO ALCOHOLISM

No one disputes the fact that children are innocent victims of alcoholism. Physical and emotional damage is inflicted which may not be recognized until later. Children of alcoholics are in high risk of developing alcoholism and a variety of emotional problems later in life. Not all children who are developing problems exhibit these problems in childhood. Therefore, every child of every alcoholic needs help.

The dysfunctional feelings going on in the family are transmitted to the child in a variety of ways. From the alcoholic the child may receive inconsistency and fear of crisis; from the nonalcoholic the child may receive fear, confusion, resentment. The alcoholic may neglect the child to drink; the nonalcoholic may neglect the child to worry.

Children respond to alcoholism in the family in a number of ways. Some children aid and protect the nondrinking spouse; some defend the alcoholic. Some attempt to stop or control the drinking. Many blame themselves. Many become nervous and troubled and have problems in other ways, perhaps in school.

Children develop their own ways of coping and surviving in the alcoholic home. They develop strengths that protect them and give them a sense of worth. These strengths are assets in childhood but may be problems later in life. Claudia Black, from her work with children of alcoholics, describes three types of seemingly well-adjusted children of alcoholics.

Some children become *superachievers.* They assume

added responsibilities at home, make excellent grades at school, become leaders, and provide structure for the rest of the family.

The second type of child is the *adjustor,* the child who rolls with the punches and doesn't get upset easily, does not express a lot of feelings, follows directions easily, and is very flexible.

The third type is the *placating* child who smooths things over in the family, tries to alleviate guilt of other family members, and is very sensitive to the feelings of others.

A sense of worth develops around a child's ability to fulfill these roles. These children are not seen as problem children but as healthy and functional. Later in life they find that everything is not all right. They did not learn to experience anger and sadness. Expressing feelings in childhood did not help them to cope. Their emotions were ignored or punished. And as adults they are unable to express feelings and are perhaps unable to feel. Superachieving children have a need to control in order to feel a sense of worth. Children who have been adjustors continue the role in adulthood. They allow themselves to be manipulated by other people which brings about a loss of self-worth and loss of control over their own lives. The placating child may never overcome the need to take care of others and to meet the needs of other people. This child may never recognize that he has needs of his own.

Children of alcoholics become 50 to 60% of society's alcoholics. This may be because of the genetic factor. Alcoholism runs in families and there is much evidence that it is hereditary. These children may be born with a predisposition for alcoholism, but research indicates that there are environmental factors that may influence whether or not the predisposition develops into alcoholism.

There is research that indicates that families who maintain structure in their family life are more likely to lower the risk of alcoholism in the next generation. Families who kept their rituals intact — such as bedtime rituals, mealtime rituals, holiday rituals, vacation rituals, religious rituals — in spite of alcoholism or alcoholic behavior were less likely to transmit alcoholism to their children.[1]

Another method of reducing the risk of transmitting alcoholism is education. Children can be taught about alcoholism and that they are in risk of developing it. They can be taught early warning signs so that they can recognize the signs when they begin to occur in their lives.

They can also be taught about alcoholism in relation to a drinking parent. They can learn that it is a disease and learn constuctive ways of reacting just as the spouse can. They need to be taught that they are not responsible. Children do not know what is going on. Lies are more frightening than the truth. They can be taught that some seemingly harsh behavior directed toward the alcoholic by the nonalcoholic may be a kindness.

Here are some rules for the nonalcoholic spouse to remember in dealing with children.

---

[1]Aldoory, Shirley, Research Into Family Factors In Alcoholism, *Alcohol Health and Research World*. Summer, 1979.

Family Recovery, Growing Beyond Addiction

1. Children often have a natural tolerance and compassion for the alcoholic. Help them to use it constructively.

2. Do not use children to help control drinking.

3. Do not try to control children's behavior so as not to trigger drinking.

4. Don't argue with the alcoholic or unburden about the alcoholic in front of them or use them as confidants.

5. Protect children from abuse — by legal means if necessary.

6. Don't try to alienate the child from the alcoholic.

7. Don't protect the child from the alcoholic unnecessarily.

8. Try to keep communication open with children by discussing alcoholism openly and allowing them to freely express their feelings.
   Children also need support outside the family. Individual or group therapy may be helpful as well as participating in Alatot and Alateen where they will have the opportunity to interact with other children or teens who have similar experiences.

SERENITY AND COURAGE

In Alanon you will often hear the Serenity Prayer: "God grant me the serenity to accept the things I cannot change; courage to change the things I can; and the wisdom to know the difference."

This seems like a simple prayer, but there is a lot involved here:

1. Learn to distinguish between what you can change and what you can't change.

2. Develop the faith necessary to accept what cannot be changed.

3. Develop the faith and courage for creative change.

4. Develop the skill to change what you can.

Sometimes we get hung up on the acceptance part of the Serenity Prayer and think we have to accept everything as it is, and we don't make the effort to distinguish what can be changed from what can't. And we never develop the courage and skills to do anything about those things we should not accept.

One of the most important things for family members of alcoholics to learn is to apply all of these steps in their lives whether the alcoholic is still drinking or recovering. One thing you must learn is that you cannot control the drinking or drinking behavior of the alcoholic. You cannot change what happens in the body of the alcoholic when he drinks. Alcoholism can only be controlled by abstinence, and abstinence is not something the family can do for the alcoholic.

You can, however, change the way you react to alcoholism, drinking, and drinking behavior. You can change your response so that alcoholism does not have to be so destructive.

And you can do something for yourself; not something *about* yourself but *for* yourself. You can develop inner strengths through personal growth to help you more effectively manage your life, and you can find supports for outer strength.

One of the most important aspects of your life that you can change is what you do to motivate the alcoholic to seek treatment. It is true that you can't control the alcoholic's drinking, but it is a misconception that an alcoholic cannot be helped until he wants help. You can do this most effectively by allowing the alcoholic to experience the consequences of his behavior even when it is painful, *particularly* when it is painful.

Sometimes acceptance of what you cannot change brings about change. This often happens when you allow the alcoholic to take responsibility for his own life and specifically for his drinking. Sometimes the spouse assumes responsibility for the alcoholic to protect the rest of the family, but it really doesn't. Sometimes spouses assume consequences for the drinker in order to deny the reality of the problem. If no one knows about it, maybe it isn't there. If there aren't any consequences, maybe the problem doesn't exist. Somehow the spouse believes that this will be the last time, it won't happen again, and everything will be all right. So they cover and they carry the responsibility the alcoholic should be carrying.

Know what you are responsible to change and what someone else is responsible to change. *You can't grow for someone else.* Grow for yourself.

Sometimes the serenity to accept requires risks and, sometimes the courage to change requires risks. It takes courage to risk your husband's job by refusing to cover for him to his boss. It takes courage to risk your pride by refusing to cover for him with the neighbors. But without that courage you cannot bring about positive change. It takes faith to allow a newly recovering alcoholic to take responsibility for the family finances for the first time. Or for you to relinquish some roles that were assumed when the alcoholic was incapable of fulfilling them. But without that faith the recovering person can't grow and progress in recovery. You may have to risk short-term comfort for long-term benefits.

It takes faith to "turn it over," an Alanon saying that applies to what you can't change. It means letting go of things and turning them over to a Power outside of yourself. It takes real faith to turn it over. It takes faith that there is a Power that can change things that you can't. It may mean turning it over to a doctor or a counselor or to God. It may mean trusting the support of AA, Alanon, or a treatment program.

But there is another kind of faith that is the courage to risk change. Just as a spouse of a drinking alcoholic may have to risk pride, security, and home to allow the alcoholic to suffer the consequences of drinking behavior, the spouse of a recovering alcoholic may have to risk in order to allow the recovering person to assume the responsibilities in the family that he has not assumed before.

It may help you to be able to distinguish the things in your life that you can change from those you can't if you take a blank piece of paper and draw three columns. Call the first one *"things I can't change,"* the second one, *"things I can change,"* and the third one *"things I am willing to change."*

BUILDING PERSONAL STRENGTHS

Before the family unit can recover, individual family members have to recover. They must develop personal strengths before they are able to motivate the alcoholic to seek treatment or to facilitate recovery of the total family unit. There should be a period of time when each member of the family is free to focus on self and do what is necessary for personal recovery. The alcoholic might receive help in a treatment program or in AA; children might receive help in group therapy or Alateen; the spouse may go to Alanon, counseling, or an educational program. Here are some tools for building your own strengths.

PROBLEM SOLVING

During the period of time that you have been immobilized by the crisis of alcoholism, you have lost the ability to solve problems without feeling a great deal of anxiety and stress. Learning some problem-solving skills will give you confidence and courage to handle problems in your life as they arise. Here is a standard problem-solving process that you may find helpful.

Step 1: **PROBLEM IDENTIFICATION:** First you have to identify what is causing difficulty. What is the problem?

Step 2: **PROBLEM CLARIFICATION:** Be specific and complete. Is this the real problem or is there a more fundamental problem?

Step 3: *IDENTIFICATION OF ALTERNATIVES:* What are your options for dealing with the problem? List them on paper so you can readily see them. Try to list at least five possible solutions. This will give you more chance of choosing the best solution and give you some alternatives if your first choice doesn't work.

Step 4: *PROJECTED CONSEQUENCES OF EACH ALTERNATIVE:* What are the probable outcomes of each option? Ask yourself these three questions: What is the *best* possible thing that could happen if I choose this alternative? What is the *worst* possible thing that could happen? What is the *most likely* thing that will happen?

Step 5: *DECISION:* Which option offers the best outcomes and seems to be the most reasonable choice for a solution? Make a decision based upon the alternatives you have.

Step 6: *ACTION:* Once you have decided on a solution to the problem you need to plan how you will carry it out. Making a plan answers the question, "What am I going to do about it?" A plan is a road map to achieve a goal. There are long-range goals and short-range goals. Long-range goals are achieved with short-range goals. One step at a time.

Step 7: *FOLLOW-UP:* Carry out your plan and evaluate how it is working.

LEARNING TO DO SOMETHING FOR YOURSELF

You may have been so caught up with the problems of your life and the needs of other people that you may have forgotten how to take care of your own needs and to do constructive things for yourself. Begin by selecting an activity that you would like to do for yourself in the near future and on a regular basis. This may be going shopping with a friend or having lunch with a friend; it may be taking a course in a subject of interest to you. Perhaps you would like to learn a new skill — to sew, to bowl, to golf. Perhaps you just need to take time for quiet periods in your life, to read or to think. Make a commitment to yourself to begin now doing something *for* yourself on a regular basis. Write down and plan how you will make this happen in your life.

You may also have forgotten how to protect your own rights, to be able to say NO at appropriate times, to recognize when others may be taking advantage of you. You need to give yourself permission to be more firm in accepting your own needs and not allowing other people and situations to push you into reactions that are not in your best interest. Respecting your own needs and rights and expecting others to respect your rights, as you respect theirs, will help you become stronger and more confident. You have the right to be treated with respect, have and express feelings and opinions, say no, make mistakes, say "I don't know," make your own choices, and ask for what you want.

Other people, of course, have the same rights, and as you respect the rights of others, you will be more comfortable in expecting them to respect yours.

SELF-PROTECTION AND CRISIS PLANNING

When living with alcoholism the unexpected becomes expected. You need to plan to protect yourself and your children from unexpected situations that could hurt you and them physically and emotionally. It is important to plan for crisis and the unexpected.

Do you know what you will do to protect yourself and your children if the alcoholic in your family becomes violent? Will you leave, call the police, call a friend, lock yourselves safely in a room? How you plan for that event could protect you from physical harm.

Do you know how to protect your family financially if it is necessary to separate from the alcoholic?

Do you know what you can expect from the police in your neighborhood should you call them in an emergency? Do you always have transportation available in an emergency? Have you checked your legal rights in case of separation, in case of physical danger, in case of financial problems, in case of destructive behavior by the alcoholic for which you might be held responsible? Do you know a medical doctor who understands the situation in your home and who might be of assistance to you when needed? Do you know if you have hospitalization or health insurance available when needed? Does it cover treatment for alcoholism? Under what circumstances? Do you know what alcoholism treatment is available to you should your alcoholic require or request it unexpectedly?

PERSONAL RELAPSE PREVENTION PLANNING

Remember that the illness of the family member is a chronic condition and subject to relapse. Without ongoing treatment and proper care of yourself, old feelings and emotions that you thought were under control may surface and get out of control. You must plan for your own relapse in order to prevent it. Relapse is a process that occurs over a period of time; it doesn't just happen. There are warning signs before relapse occurs. There are situations that trigger out-of-control behavior. Here is a list of warning signs that might trigger relapse, compiled by a number of recovering spouses of alcoholics. Identify those that apply to you.

1. Fatigue or lack of rest.

2. Problems with children.

3. Feeling sorry for yourself.

4. Not taking time to do things for yourself.

5. Trying to control behavior of other people.

6. Missing Alanon meetings.

7. Discontinuing personal treatment.

8. Blaming others.

9. Irritability.

10. Indecision.

11. Not making plans.

12. Not following through with plans.

Add others that you can think of. Once you have identified those things that might trigger relapse in your own life, then decide what you will do to interrupt that process the next time it occurs. For example, if you recognize that fatigue or lack of rest is especially important on your list, decide what you will do the next time you are aware that you are not getting enough rest. Perhaps it is not a matter of choice. Perhaps a situation interferes with proper rest, such as the sickness of a child or other unexpected family situation. In that case you may ask a relative or friend to help you out, or if that is impossible, maybe you just need extra emotional support during that time. Perhaps just talking with a friend or going to an Alanon meeting might give you the extra strength necessary to make it through a difficult time.

Take a piece of paper, list your personal warning signs of relapse, and beside each one indicate what you will do the next time it occurs.

LEARNING TO HELP THE ALCOHOLIC

Intervention is interruption of the disease process in the alcoholic by concerned persons. Because denial of the disease is part of the disease, most alcoholics are unable to interrupt the process themselves. So it is necessary for concerned persons to take steps to facilitate intervention. There are a variety of methods and techniques that you can use to motivate the alcoholic you are concerned about to get help. All of them should be done with the guidance of a professional counselor who will work with you and teach you how to intervene.

Before they can recover, alcoholics must come to believe they are ill. Pain is nature's way of convincing us we are ill. But alcoholics are able to avoid pain by:

1. adapting to the symptoms of the disease,
2. blackouts which erase unpleasant experiences from memory,
3. their denial symptoms which allow them to block reality from conscious awareness,
4. continued alcohol consumption used to escape painful reality.

Even when the pain of alcoholism is intense, the alcoholic does not have an awareness of the source of the pain. The need to drink plus an impaired nervous system which distorts thinking keeps the alcoholic from associating drinking with pain.

The intent of intervention is to (1) intensify the pain of drinking above the pain of not drinking and (2) produce within the alcoholic the awareness that drinking is the source of pain.

This means that you stop protecting the alcoholic from the consequences of his own behavior. It means that you begin appropriately confronting him with evidence of his alcohol-related behavior in such a way that he must begin to see the reality of his situation. You must be willing to take the drinking problems out of the closet and acknowledge to yourself, the alcoholic, and the rest of the family that there is a problem. You must stop pretending that everything is all right or that it will be all right if you can just hang on awhile longer or if you can just get through the immediate crisis.

You must bring the problem out in the open so that the alcoholic can become painfully aware of it. This may be the only way to save his life and your family.

The goal of intervention is treatment. It is not to get the alcoholic to stop drinking. Under pressure most alcoholics will agree to stop drinking (if only to prove they are not alcoholic so they can drink). But sooner or later they will drink again unless they have treatment. The goal of an intervention is to motivate the alcoholic to seek treatment. Treatment can be private counseling, inpatient treatment, outpatient treatment, or AA.

OBSTACLES AND RESISTANCE TO INTERVENTION

Many people believe alcoholics must *hit bottom* before they can be helped. This is not true if you mean they must get down and out, as low as they can get. Many alcoholics seek help long before they reach that point. No matter where they are in the progression of their disease, they almost never receive the insight that they need treatment without some outside motivation. The sooner that motivation comes, the better chance there is for full recovery. The later it comes the more risk there is that the alcoholic may die first or that there may be physical or mental impairment so severe that it is irreparable or will interfere with recovery.

Let me give you another definition of hitting bottom. When the alcoholic hits this point it is probable help will be accepted. Think of hitting bottom as that point at which the pain of drinking becomes more intense than the pain of not drinking. People concerned about the alcoholic can help that point come sooner than later.

It is a common belief that the alcoholic must want help in order for treatment to be effective. The truth is that alcoholics successfully recover after accepting treatment for many other reasons than a personal desire for recovery. The pressure to get treatment or lose their jobs motivates many alcoholics to get help. The possible loss of a marriage, child, or other important relationship is strong motivation for others. The risk of losing something they value more than drinking gets them into treatment, and the treatment process itself brings an insight into the personal need for recovery. The role of family and friends is to motivate the alcoholic to seek treatment, and then trust the treatment process to motivate the alcoholic to want recovery.

Some people interpret the Alanon principles of acceptance and detachment to mean that no one must ever interfere in the alcoholic's life for any reason. Remember the Serenity Prayer doesn't end after "accept the things I cannot change." It goes on to say, "courage to change the things I can." You cannot control the drinking or drinking behavior, but you can help motivate the alcoholic to do something about it himself. Have the courage to change what you can.

Sometimes an intervention seems cruel. Remember that intervention is not something you are doing *to* the alcoholic. It is something you are doing *for* him. It may be the most caring thing you have ever done. It may save his life.

Fear is a frequent block to effective intervention — fear of losing financial security or status in the community, fear of losing the emotional support or affection of the alcoholic, fear of failure, fear of reprisal from the alcoholic, fear of change or of the unknown. These are normal and understandable fears, and no one but you can decide if the possibility of recovery is worth the risk. Remember, however, that alcoholism is a progressive disease. As it progresses, the things you fear will probably happen anyway. It will get worse, and the longer it goes on, the greater the risk.

It is wise to look at the risks involved in an intervention process. There is a need for caution. Always proceed with an intervention with the guidance of a professional person who has knowledge of intervention techniques. Assess your own ability and willingness to follow through with an intervention once you begin. Harm can come from an intervention begun and not completed. Enter into the intervention out of caring, not anger or resentment or a desire to get even. If your behavior is intended to hurt the alcoholic rather than help, it is not an intervention; it is revenge.

THE INTERVENTION PROCESS

Following are the basic steps of intervention.

Assessment

The first step in making any change is determining what really needs to be changed. A counselor should help you determine whether drinking is the primary source of problems within your family or whether the family dysfunction is actually due to some other cause. The counselor can also help you assess the level of personal strength of family members and the ability of the family to work together throughout the intervention process. Based upon this assessment the counselor can help you develop an intervention plan that is appropriate for the needs and resouces of your family.

Preparation

1. Develop your own personal strengths. Focus on your own recovery before you focus on the recovery of the alcoholic. Develop the confidence and ability to handle your own life and the courage and skill to intervene in the disease process of the loved one.

2. Interrupt your controlling behavior. Stop attempting to control drinking, the reasons for drinking, or drinking behavior. Those things you can't change. Let go of them.

3. Interrupt your enabling behavior. Don't make it easy for the alcoholic to continue drinking. Let the alcoholic experience the natural consequences of drinking. Don't protect, cover up, rescue, or get drawn into alibis and excuses.

4. Learn about intervention techniques. Discuss with your counselor various methods and their appropriateness for your situation.

5. Explore the potential benefits and risks of intervention for the family. Take whatever steps are necessary to protect the family physically, emotionally, financially, and legally. When dealing with alcoholism, the risk of violence must always be considered and protective precautions taken.

6. Identify your personal obstacles or resistances to the intervention. Work through these obstacles before you begin an intervention process you may not be able to complete.

7. Make a firm decision and commitment to intervention and to bringing about recovery in the person you love.

8. Make a plan with your counselor as to exactly how the intervention will be carried out.

Invitation To The Alcoholic

Let the alcoholic know you are getting counseling and invite him or her to join you. If he accepts, the other intervention steps may not be needed.

Throughout the intervention process you should be as honest and open as possible. Let the alcoholic know that you are getting counseling and continue to issue the invitation for him or her to join you.

Behavior Awareness Feedback

Because of neurological impairment, denial, and blackouts, most alcoholics are not aware of the effect drinking is having on their lives. They are experiencing pain, but they are not aware that the pain is related to drinking. Behavior awareness feedback is intended to give alcoholics regular feedback about drinking behavior so that they are able to connect the pain in their lives with drinking.

Allow the alcoholic to experience pain. Do not control, rescue, or protect. Do not do *anything* that will reduce the pain of the consequences of drinking. Produce evidence that pain is alcohol related. Leave empty bottles, liquor receipts, pictures, etc. where the alcoholic will be aware of them. Report inappropriate behavior to the alcoholic whenever it occurs. Here are some suggestions that will help you provide this feedback.

1. Try to be calm; get rid of your own anger before reporting.

2. Choose an appropriate time and place. Don't bring it up at the breakfast table when the children are asking for lunch money and looking for their books.

3. Use "I" language when possible. This means speaking from your own perspective, "I was frightened," or "I was embarrassed," not "you were," or "you did."

4. State circumstances simply. Don't overkill; don't preach or coax; don't get into name calling or garbage dumping. Be firm and matter of fact. "I was concerned when you didn't come home in time to take Bobby to the game as you promised. He was disappointed and cried. We were both hurt when you came home drunk, saying you had to work late."

5. Don't become defensive. Don't react to the alcoholic's reaction. The alcoholic may become angry and accusing. There is no need to respond or defend yourself. You have reported what you needed to report, and there is no need to say more.

6. Communicate caring. "I am concerned about your health," or "I am afraid you might get hurt."

7. Do not use the word "alcoholic." You are only trying to bring about an awareness that help is needed. Let a professional make a diagnosis.

Crisis Is Opportunity

Crisis brings pain. Pain is your method of communicating that the alcoholic needs help. *Crisis is your opportunity.* You can use it for your purpose. Take advantage of it to motivate the alcoholic to get treatment. Here are some guidelines to help you use crisis effectively.

1. Identify potential crises that could occur for your alcoholic and decide what you can do to utilize them when they occur.

2. Be prepared. The opportunity of crisis will be of no value if you are not prepared to utilize it as fully as possible. Know what treatment facilities are available. Know what your hospitalization will pay (or won't pay) for alcoholism treatment. Know a doctor that you can turn to when you need to. Know what assistance you can expect from the police in your area in certain situations. Line up some support. Make arrangements ahead of time with someone to help you in the event you need help; a friend, a counselor, someone from AA.

3. When a crisis occurs, intensify it for the alcoholic, not for the rest of the family. What is a crisis for the alcoholic does not need to be a crisis for everyone.

4. Provide strong direction to the person as to what can be done about the situation (direct toward treatment).

5. Use leverage. At this point the alcoholic may be willing to cooperate or bargain to avoid the pain of the crisis.

Use that. Offer treatment as the way out. Talk to his boss and see if he will give back the job if he gets treatment. Post bond only if he gets treatment. Refuse to do anything that might help unless he gets treatment.

Network Confrontation

If the alcoholic does not agree to treatment because of the change in the family, behavior awareness feedback, or as a result of a crisis, a network confrontation should be considered. This method is explained by Vernon Johnson in the book, *I'll Quit Tomorrow*. With this technique the family presents an overwhelming case of objective evidence that there is a drinking problem and they urge treatment. The purpose is to allow the alcoholic to see reality and accept the need for help.

A group of people that are meaningful to the alcoholic compile and present to him individual lists of facts and data that strongly indicate a problem with alcohol.

The data presented should be specific and descriptive of events which have occurred or conditions which exist. The descriptions should be first-hand accounts, free of opinions and generalizations. The tone should be caring and nonjudgmental, and the evidence should be tied directly into drinking.

The group urges the alcoholic to get help and offers treatment alternatives. This method should be undertaken with the help of a professional and after reading about the technique in the book, *I'll Quit Tomorrow*. It should be practiced in advance with a professional.

Imposition Of Consequences

At times even the network confrontation fails to cause the alcoholic to get help. At this point the family members may need to use leverage to force the alcoholic to choose between drinking and other things he values. The consequences that are imposed may increase in pressure over a period of time if there is no response. The family may withhold money or financial support. Or they may withhold companionship or support. It may be necessary for the family to separate from the alcoholic until he agrees to get treatment. There is probably something the person values more than drinking and when forced to choose, will choose to give up drinking rather than lose what he values more.

Family Recovery

Whether or not the alcoholic gets treatment as a result of the intervention, your family life will change. The family will either begin recovering with the alcoholic or in spite of the alcoholic. The real tasks of recovery begin rather than end with intervention.

UNDERSTANDING THE RECOVERY PROCESS IN THE ALCOHOLIC

Sometimes the family expects that as soon as the alcoholic gets treatment that everything will be all right. There are a number of sobriety-based symptoms of alcoholism that the family needs to understand. Understanding what is going on will enable you to be more supportive, but it will also help you to know what you can reasonably expect from the alcoholic.

POST ACUTE WITHDRAWAL SYNDROME

Post acute withdrawal syndrome is a group of symptoms resulting from neurological (brain and central nervous system) impairments that persist into recovery. Post acute withdrawal surfaces 7 to 14 days into abstinence, grows to a peak intensity over the next three to six months, and may last up to two years.

The post acute withdrawal syndrome affects thought processes, emotional processes, and memory. Symptoms include problems with abstract thinking, concentration, and memory. The alcoholic also becomes stress sensitive. There is an overreaction and lowered tolerance to stress.

Intelligence is not affected. It is as if the computer in the head is not functioning properly. The impairment can be corrected, but it takes time and it takes some effort. The paradox of recovery is that recovery from neurological impairment requires abstinence, but the impairment interferes with the ability to abstain. This means that everything possible must be done to control the effects of PAW while recovery is taking place.

There is a direct relationship between elevated stress and the severity of PAW. Each tends to reinforce the other. Stress aggravates PAW and makes it more severe; the intensity of PAW creates stress which further aggravates PAW. Recovering alcoholics can learn to identify sources of stress and develop skills in decision making and problem solving to help reduce stress. Proper diet, exercise, regular habits, and positive attitudes all play an important part in controlling PAW. Relaxation can be used as a tool to retrain the brain to function properly and to reduce stress. Learning about post acute withdrawal symptoms, knowing what to expect, and not overreacting to the symptoms increase the ability to function appropriately and effectively. Remember the symptoms of PAW will pass with continued sobriety.

STATE DEPENDENT LEARNING

Much of what alcoholics have learned has been while drinking. Those things are always affected by state dependent learning. What they learned while drinking they will recall most easily at the same blood alcohol level. Without alcohol they are unable to perform tasks that were easily performed while drinking and believe that alcohol improves performance. As alcohol is used with more life activities, it becomes more difficult for alcoholics to function without it.

Let's suppose Mary has been drinking when she first learns to dance. She later tries to dance while totally sober. She can't quite recall how she did it. She remembers learning, but the actual performance skills are not there. She tries it again while drinking and it all comes back. She dances beautifully. The same thing occurs with bowling, sex, social skills. Job-related skills are not so frequently associated with alcohol, so the job may be the last affected by drinking. Other skills may become totally dependent upon alcohol.

Sober alcoholics feel they should be able to do these things because they have done them many times before. But when they attempt to accomplish them without alcohol, they can't do them in spite of their efforts. They feel that there is something is wrong with them, that they are crazy or incompetent. A minor limitation is turned into a major crippler. They believe they cannot perform and become very embarrassed and humiliated. As a result they avoid situations in which relearning can take place.

Understanding what is going on and support from the family may be all that is necessary to give the alcoholic the courage to relearn these skills. It has been demonstrated that skills that are learned state dependently can be relearned rapidly through structured practice.

A NEW LIFESTYLE

The recovering alcoholic has to develop a new lifestyle in order to maintain sobriety. A way of life centered around drinking will not maintain sobriety. The alcoholic must develop new patterns of living, build new friendships, find new sources of recreation and leisure, find his place within the family, and learn to communicate in new ways.

Change, even positive change, is stress producing. The recovering alcoholic is encountering much change all at once. Most alcoholism therapists advise against any unnecessary major change for a year; that is, a major move, change of jobs, major educational decision, marriage, etc. Support from the family is helpful throughout the necessary change that comes with recovery.

FAMILY RECOVERY

Once family members have had a period of time to focus on their own recovery—the alcoholic has had treatment and other family members have had education, therapy, and an opportunity to build some personal strengths—you are ready to focus on recovery of the family unit. Full recovery for everyone comes from a healthy family system.

THE FAMILY AS A SYSTEM

A system is a number of parts that work together for a specific outcome. A change in one part will affect the balance of the system. The rest of the system will compensate to balance itself. What has happened in the alcoholic family is that alcoholism has affected the balance of the family system, and the family members have attempted to rebalance around the alcoholism. When recovery of the parts has occurred, there is a need to rebalance the system around recovery.

This may not be easy. Much has changed. Family *rules* have changed to survive alcoholism. Some rules that you may have developed to cope with drinking may be:

Keep the noise down when Dad is home so not to upset him.

Don't talk about drinking.

Don't tell Grandma that Mom has been drinking.

Family Recovery, Growing Beyond Addiction

Don't expect too much, you may be disappointed.

Don't ask questions.

Don't express feelings, you may be punished.

These rules may not have been spoken, but they have kept the family functioning. Now new rules are needed for a healthy family.

Family *roles* have changed. In order to maintain the family when some parts were dysfunctional, roles have been switched. Perhaps:

Mom is working and Dad is at home (he can't keep a job).

Dad is working two jobs (to pay the extra bills or to escape the chaos at home while Mom drinks).

The oldest child is cooking, cleaning, and caring for the other kids (because one parent is drinking and the other immobilized by pain).

Family *rituals* have changed. The family activities have been restructured to accommodate drinking. Mealtimes, bedtimes, holiday and vacation activity, leisure activities, traditions, routines have all been changed because drinking behavior has interferred or because of inconsistency due to drinking.

Family *communication* has changed. If life becomes centered around alcoholism, what is there to talk about but alcoholism — directly or indirectly? Chances are you have not been talking about it directly, maybe not even consciously thinking about it. But you have been thinking and talking about the resulting behaviors and situations. Communication has become accusatory or defensive. Verbal communication may have almost ceased because everyone has been afraid to talk about what they are really feeling. The communication that has existed has been manipulated for self-protection of the family members.

RESTRUCTURING RULES, ROLES, AND RITUALS

You can't go back to the way you were. This may be your most difficult hurdle. Some of the family may want the same rules, roles, and rituals that existed before. Others may want to keep things as they are. Neither will work productively. You have all changed and you can't go back. And you can't keep things as they are because rules, roles, and rituals developed to maintain a system organized around disease cannot maintain a system organized around health. But strengths used to maintain that system can be used in recovery.

The recovering alcoholic needs and usually wants to resume responsibilities within the family. Other family members may be reluctant to allow that for a variety of reasons. They may be comfortable in performing those tasks themselves. Or it may take time for them to believe that they can really depend on the alcoholic. Children who have assumed adult roles may have their sense of identity and self-worth tied up in those roles.

Mutual respect, trust, patience, consideration, and time will be needed. It is not necessary that everyone give up new functions they have assumed and go back to the old structure. The old structure may not have been very healthy either. A wife may have gone to work and now finds that she enjoys that role and wants to continue it. The family can accommodate that in restructuring.

Family Recovery, Growing Beyond Addiction

In order to restructure roles, rules, and rituals, the family members must learn to talk to each other. New communication skills are necessary in order to share what each is feeling, to listen to one another, to discuss alternatives, and make decisions that affect the whole family. Communication skills don't just happen. They develop with practice. It may be helpful to go to a professional who can teach you some good communication skills, and then, like most everything else, you learn it by doing it.

The family needs to be free to restructure according to the needs of individual members. Rules, roles, and rituals are negotiable when the system is not threatened by change. A family that provides freedom within limits can offer stability and freedom at the same time. To every member it can offer space to grow.

BIBLIOGRAPHY

Ackerman, Robert J., *Children Of Alcoholics.* Holmes Beach, Florida, Learning Publications, 1978.

Aldoory, Shirley, Research Into Family Factors In Alcoholism, *Alcohol Health and Research World.* Summer, 1979.

Black, Claudia, *It Will Never Happen To Me.* Denver, M.A.C. Printing and Publications, 1981.

Budenz, Daniel T., *The Family Illness Of Alcohol/Drug Dependency.* Middleton, Wisconsin, Progressive Literature, 1979.

Cross, Wilbur, *Kids and Booze.* New York, E.P. Dutton, 1979.

Dyer, Wayne W., *Pulling Your Own Strings.* New York, Avon, 1979.

Fajardo, Roque, *Helping Your Alcoholic Before He Or She Hits Bottom.* New York, Crown Publishers, 1976.

Goodwin, Donald W., *Is Alcoholism Hereditary?* New York, Oxford University Press, 1976.

Howard, Don and Nancy, *A Family Approach To Problem Drinking.* Columbia, Missouri, Family Training Center, 1976.

Family Recovery, Growing Beyond Addiction

Johnson, Vernon, *I'll Quit Tomorrow.* New York, Harper & Row, 1973.

Kellerman, Joseph L., *A Guide For The Family Of The Alcoholic.* Alanon Family Groups.

Maxwell, Ruth, *The Booze Battle.* New York, Praser Publishers, 1976.

McCabe, Thomas R., *Victims No More.* Hazelden, 1978.

McWilliams, James J., *Tough Love.* Kansas City, National Council On Alcoholism, 1978.

Miller, Merlene; Gorski, Terence T., and Miller, David K., *Learning To Live Again, A Guide For Recovery From Alcoholism.* Independence, Missouri, Independence Press, 1982.

Satir, Virginia, *Peoplemaking.* Palo Alto, California, Science and Behavior Books, Inc., 1972.

Wegscheider, Don and Sharon, *Family Illness: Chemical Dependency.* Crystal, Minnesota, Nurturing Networks, 1978.

Wegscheider, Sharon, *Another Chance.* Palo Alto, California, Science and Behavior Books, Inc., 1981.

OTHER PUBLICATIONS BY THE AUTHORS

Learning To Live Again—A Guide For Recovery From Alcoholism
Merlene Miller, Terence T. Gorski, David K. Miller

Family Recovery—Growing Beyond Addiction
Merlene Miller and Terence T. Gorski

Staying Sober—A Guide for Relapse Prevention
Terence T. Gorski and Merlene Miller

These books are available from
Herald House-Independence Press

TRAINING IN RELAPSE PREVENTION

Relapse prevention planning is a skill that requires training, practice, and supervision. Most agencies are not equipped to effectively train or supervise staff in these methods. Since relapse prevention planning is such a specialty, CENAPS Corporation offers professional training through workshops and inservice training. CENAPS Corporation will also open a Center for Relapse Prevention within a treatment center or private practice. If an agency opens a Center for Relapse Prevention, CENAPS Corporation will train and supervise the staff, develop patient care protocols and patient record systems, and link these systems into an applied research network.

For information contact

CENAPS Corporation
P.O. Box 184
Hazel Crest, Illinois
60429
(708) 335-3606